SCOTT JOPLIN

ONE HUNDRED YEARS ON

SARAH PEACE

HUGH C. SHIELDS

SCOTT JOPLIN: ONE HUNDRED YEARS ON

Second Edition
This edition is written and formatted in standard British
English. Readers may notice regional variations in
spelling and punctuation.

First published in Great Britain in 2017 by DoubleU,
an imprint of LibraryX.

Cover design: SP

A catalogue record for this book is available from the
British Library.

ISBN-13: 978-0-9931751-3-8
ISBN-10: 0993175139

"A man's character is the element of his success, as it is the attribute of his power. To be his own master, he must first be a master of himself."

— Frederick Douglass, *Self-Made Men (1872)*

CONTENTS

Scott Joplin is hailed worldwide as the "King of Ragtime," a pioneer whose syncopated rhythms ignited a musical revolution at the turn of the twentieth century. This title is well deserved, yet it often obscures the true depth of his contribution to American culture. This concise tribute, published to coincide with the one hundredth anniversary of his death in April 1917, seeks to right that imbalance.

It so happened that the day we began work on this essay, 21st March, was itself significant in the civil rights movement. For it was on this day in 1965 that Martin Luther King Jr. and a number of other activists and supporters began a five-day freedom march from Selma to Montgomery in Alabama. While that historic march is a well-known pillar of the American story, the life of the Ragtime King often remains on the periphery.

What stands out in Joplin's story is a resolute belief in the power of knowledge. While he is remembered today at festivals in Missouri and by enthusiasts across the globe, his legacy feels incomplete without a full understanding of his work in grand opera. His masterpiece, *Treemonisha*, represents a vision of hope that remains strikingly relevant a century later. But is Joplin's legacy wholly fulfilled?

Joplin once predicted that he would be recognised twenty-five years after his death. Now, more than a century later, this essay asserts that his true legacy is found in his vision of a progressive and positive future, a vision that proves the human spirit, fired by creativity and the quest for knowledge, is the most powerful tool for liberation.

The quest to fully realise Joplin's vision is still ongoing. It is a puzzle where the final, most significant pieces are only now being put into place by a new generation of musicians and scholars. It is no exaggeration to describe the scale of his talent as that of an invisible genius. This tribute is a call to return that genius to the spotlight where it belongs.

Hugh C. Shields
London, 2016

INTRODUCTION
A SILENT ARCHITECT OF THE AMERICAN PULSE

The history of American music is often told as a series of fortunate accidents, a spontaneous collision of cultures in the saloons of the South or the sitting rooms of the North. Yet, at the centre of this narrative stands a figure whose life was anything but accidental. Scott Joplin did not merely stumble upon the rhythms that would define a century; he engineered them. He was a man who understood, with a clarity that bordered on the prophetic, that technical mastery was the only currency that could reliably bypass the blockades of a segregated society.

In 1872, Frederick Douglass argued that success was an attribute of power derived from self-mastery. Three decades later, Joplin would embody this philosophy in the most unlikely of arenas: the gritty world of ragtime. While his contemporaries saw a popular fad, Joplin saw a complex, formal language of American classical music. He was the "Invisible Genius" because his most significant labour was often unseen, conducted in the quiet hours of study, in the meticulous notation of scores, and in the unwavering belief that his "Human Capital" was his greatest route to freedom.

This essay is an investigation into that labour. It is a

study of a man who refused to be defined by the "shroud of obscurity" cast by his era. By examining Joplin through the lens of pragmatic excellence and intellectual self-reliance, we begin to see a composer who was more than a musician. He was a philosopher of the keyboard, a strategist of the archive, and a pioneer of the idea that true liberation begins within the disciplined architecture of the mind. As we mark the centenary of his demise in 2017, we finally pull back the curtain on a legacy that was built to last for a hundred years and beyond.

CHAPTER 1
THE BORDERS OF LINDEN AND TEXARKANA

The early life of Scott Joplin is often framed as a series of geographic movements from the borderlands of Texas to the musical laboratories of Sedalia, Missouri. However, the most significant journey Joplin undertook was internal. It was a disciplined migration from the raw talent of a natural musician to the rigorous, self-imposed standards of a formal composer. In an era where the social and economic mobility of Black Americans was systematically throttled, Joplin identified a singular, portable asset that no legislation could confiscate: his own human capital.

This chapter examines the formative years of the Invisible Genius through the lens of radical self-reliance. While the world around him debated the merits of industrial versus classical education, Joplin moved quietly toward a synthesis of both. He understood that to compete in the markets of the world, as Booker T. Washington advocated, he had to produce a product of undeniable excellence. His apprenticeship was not merely musical; it was a strategic accumulation of intellectual property.

We explore how his early encounters with German classical theory provided the architectural scaffolding for his syncopated innovations. By mastering the rules of the Western canon, Joplin gained the authority to break them with precision. This was not an act of assimilation, but an act of sovereign creation. He was building a foundation that would allow his music to survive the ephemeral trends of the 1890s and endure as a permanent pillar of American art. As we look back today, we see that Joplin's philosophy was founded on a simple, pragmatic truth: that the most durable form of freedom is the one you build for yourself.

The Mystery of Origin: A Fragile Archive
For decades, biographers accepted November 24, 1868, as Joplin's birthdate, yet the geography of his arrival remains a point of scholarly contention. The debate centres on two Texas towns: Linden and Texarkana.

Edward Berlin, a preeminent Joplin biographer, argued persuasively for Linden in Cass County. His assertion rested on a chronological technicality: the city of Texarkana was not officially established until 1873, five years after Joplin's birth. However, this narrative was challenged in 2015 by musicologist John Tennison. Tennison's research uncovered evidence that the name "Texarkana" appeared in print and local usage as early as 1856, suggesting that a "Texarkana birth" was not a chronological impossibility but a historical reality.

This tension between official municipal records and lived oral history serves as a foundational theme for Joplin's life. If his very birthplace is subject to "ragged" interpretations, it mirrors the syncopation of his music as an insistence on existing in the spaces between the beats of established history.

The dispute between Linden and Texarkana is more than a geographic debate; it is a window into the systemic erasure that defined the post-Reconstruction South. In a society where Black lives were often recorded only through the lens of labour or criminal justice, the lack of a definitive birth record for the King of Ragtime serves as a primary example of the Invisible Genius motif.

While Edward Berlin's case for Linden rests on the rigid municipal timeline of Texarkana's incorporation, John Tennison's discovery of the name in earlier local usage highlights the importance of the oral archive, the lived memory of a community that existed before the state saw fit to document it.

The Piano as a Declaration of Dignity
The intellectual and artistic scaffolding of Joplin's genius was built within a household defined by a sharp contrast between gruelling labour and melodic richness. Born the second of six children,

Scott was the product of a unique union: his father, Giles Joplin, was a freedman from North Carolina who laboured for the railroad, while his mother, Florence Gibbons, was a freeborn woman from Kentucky who worked as a domestic cleaner.

In the Joplin home, music was the primary language of survival. Giles provided a connection to the European-influenced string traditions of the violin, while Florence brought the rhythmic vitality of the African American vocal and banjo traditions. This wasn't merely a hobby; it was a basic education in the dualities of American music. By the age of seven, Scott was already displaying a confident flair on the piano, synthesizing his father's structured lines with his mother's rhythmic spirit.

When Florence Joplin acquired a used square piano for her son in the 1880s, it was not merely a musical purchase; it was a political act. In the agrarian and industrial economy of East Texas, a piano in a Black household was a declaration of intellectual dignity. It stood in stark contrast to the gruelling physical labour performed by Giles Joplin on the railroad or Florence in the homes of white families.

This instrument represented an early commitment to the "Aesthetic Uplift." Before W.E.B. Du Bois had even codified the concept of the "Talented

Tenth," Florence Joplin was investing in the idea that high-order artistic expression was a tool of liberation. The piano allowed Scott to move beyond the coarse street traditions and begin internalising the complex harmonies of the Western world, turning his mother's sacrifice into a foundation for intellectual resistance.

The Mentor: The Symbiosis of Outsiders

The catalyst that transformed Joplin's raw talent into disciplined artistry was Julius Weiss, a German-Jewish immigrant. In the rigid racial and religious hierarchy of 1880s Texas, both the German-Jewish teacher and the young Black prodigy were "others." Weiss did not merely teach Joplin the mechanics of the piano; he introduced him to the German Romantic tradition, a philosophy that viewed music as a vehicle for national identity and spiritual transcendence.

This mentorship provided Joplin with a "Third Way" in the burgeoning debate over Black liberation. By introducing him to the works of the European masters, Weiss showed him that the operatic form and high art were not the exclusive domain of any one race. Joplin began to see the "ragged time" of the American South as a raw material that could be refined into the high art of the masters. This cross-cultural intellectual exchange suggested that the mastery of complex, world-class art forms was itself a legitimate and radical path toward equality.

The Minstrel Mask: The Double-Edged Sword

As Joplin reached his mid-teens, he began to navigate the double-edged sword of the entertainment industry. He was a student of high art who was simultaneously forced to enter the professional world through the door of minstrelsy. Performing on the street and eventually joining a Texarkana minstrel troupe in 1891 required Joplin to don a metaphorical mask, participating in a genre built on the caricature of Black life in order to fund his higher ambitions.

This economic necessity created a profound psychological friction. To gain a platform, Joplin had to navigate the "Coon Song" market, creating early works that often catered to the very stereotypes he sought to dismantle. This tax on Black creativity, which necessitated performing a stereotype to gain the resources required to subvert it would frame his later obsession with opera as a desperate attempt to achieve artistic purity.

The Geometry of the Rag: A Technical Prelude

Technically the "Invisible Genius" was already manifesting in Joplin's early experiments with ragged time. This music was a mathematical fusion of two worlds. The left hand maintained the strict and unyielding two-four time of a European march. This rhythmic foundation symbolized the rigid and structured society in which he lived. Meanwhile the right hand ragged the melody to provide a fluid and syncopated freedom. This contrast represented the Black spirit.

This architectural approach is best heard in the familiar strains of *The Entertainer*. The left hand functions as a relentless and driving heartbeat, maintaining a steady march that mirrors the mechanical pulse of the industrial age. Against this rigid backdrop the right hand offers a series of unexpected leaps. It strikes notes just a fraction of a second away from where the ear expects them to land. This creates a friction that feels both modern and rebellious. For the musician this is known as syncopation. For the social historian it is the sound of a person finding room to breathe inside a restrictive system.

This tension between the "on-beat" and the "off-beat" was the physical embodiment of the American experience. By stabilising this ragged rhythm within the formal architecture of the march, Joplin was performing a feat of cultural alchemy. He was proving that the rhythms of the street could coexist with the discipline of parlour music. By the time he looked toward Chicago and Sedalia he was not just looking for work. He was carrying a mission to prove that ragtime was not merely the indecorous chattering it was deemed. Instead he presented it as a sophisticated pillar of American high art.

CHAPTER 2

THE "BIG THREE" AND THE SEDALIA SCENE

As the nineteenth century drew to a close, Scott Joplin began to move beyond the boundaries of local performances. This period was not merely a rise to fame. It was a rigorous process of professionalisation. Joplin moved from being a wandering musician to a structured composer. He began to build a community that would define an entire American era.

The transition into a formal architect of sound began amidst the industrial energy of Chicago. The 1893 World's Fair served as a global stage where Joplin first recognised the commercial potential of syncopation. Yet, the true refinement of his vision occurred in Sedalia, Missouri. This location acted as a creative laboratory. It was here that *The Maple Leaf Rag* was forged. This publication marked the first major conversion of Joplin's intellectual labour into a protected, high-value asset.

This chapter explores how Joplin's influence expanded through mentorship and strategic association. By fostering a circle of creators in St. Louis, he effectively established a school of thought that would produce the "Big Three" of the genre. His role was not merely that of a performer. He was a curator of excellence who elevated his peers, including James Scott and Joseph Lamb. From our perspective today, this period stands as a testament to the power of collective human capital. Joplin proved that a structured movement could achieve a level of cultural permanence that individual fame alone could never guarantee.

The Chicago Years and Early Arrangements

The move to Chicago in the early 1890s marked a departure from the solo busking of his youth. Joplin arrived during the transformative energy of the 1893 World's Fair. He formed a four-piece band with a distinctive and heavy sound. The group featured a unique instrumentation of cornet, clarinet, tuba, and baritone horn. This setup was significant. It bridged the gap between the brass bands of the Victorian era and the rhythmic experiments of the new South.

In Chicago, Joplin began to demonstrate a unique ability to cross the colour line. He arranged music that appealed to both Black and white audiences without sacrificing the "ragged" integrity of his compositions. This was a strategic use of syncopation. He realized that a well-ordered rhythm could serve as a universal language. It allowed him to enter white social spaces while maintaining a distinctly African-American artistic voice.

Sedalia: The Cradle of Ragtime
While many associate Joplin with the nightlife of the district, his time in Sedalia, Missouri, was rooted in the classroom. He enrolled in music courses at the George R. Smith College for Negroes. This decision was a manifestation of his lifelong commitment to formal education. It was at this institution that he met his first wife, Belle Jones. His academic focus challenged the popular myth of the untutored musician. Joplin was an intellectual who sought to ground his folk-inspired rhythms in the deep logic of Western music theory.

Despite his academic pursuits, the physical heartbeat of his music remained the Maple Leaf Club. This establishment in Sedalia became a hub for Black social life and creative exchange. It served as the "Cradle of Ragtime." The club provided the atmosphere and the title for the work that would eventually change the landscape of global music.

The Publication of the Maple Leaf Rag
The most pivotal moment in Joplin's career occurred in a small music store in Sedalia. It was here that he met John Stillwell Stark. Stark was a white publisher who possessed a rare appreciation for the technical complexity of Joplin's work. This alliance broke the exploitative industry standards of the time. Joplin insisted on a contract that provided

him with a forward-thinking royalty agreement that was virtually unheard of for Black composers. This was a sophisticated business move that ensured his economic independence. By agreeing to a royalty-based contract rather than a flat fee, Stark acknowledged Joplin as a long-term business partner rather than a temporary employee.

The publication of *The Maple Leaf Rag* in 1899 fundamentally altered the American soundscape. It eventually sold over one million copies. The piece became the standard for Ragtime because of its technical innovation. Joplin utilised rollicking syncopation and powerful octave chord progressions. These elements elevated the genre from simple melodies to high-order compositions. For the first time, a complex work of Black genius was being played in the parlours of affluent homes across America.

Defining the "Big Three"

Joplin was not interested in being a solitary genius; he understood that for Ragtime to be taken seriously by the musical establishment, it needed to be a movement rather than a one-man show. He sought to codify a "Classical Ragtime" tradition that would outlast him. This collective legacy was cemented through the "Big Three" composers: Scott Joplin, James Scott, and Joseph Lamb. Together, they proved the genre's technical depth was a formal discipline.

Joplin's role in this trio was that of a gatekeeper and an advocate. When he met James Scott, he was immediately impressed by the younger man's talent. Joplin introduced Scott to John Stark. This led to the commercial success of the Frog Legs Rag in 1906.

Perhaps the most surprising member of the group was Joseph Lamb. As a white composer, Lamb represented the ultimate proof of Joplin's philosophy. He believed that the genre was a formal discipline that anyone could master with enough study. Joplin recognised Lamb's "melody-heavy flair." He personally recommended Lamb's work to Stark. This resulted in the publication of *Sensation* in 1908. By fostering this trio, Joplin proved that Ragtime was a legitimate school of composition.

The St. Louis Circle and Mentorship
As Joplin moved to St. Louis, his home became a hub for creative exchange. He opened his doors to aspiring young composers. He turned his private life into a public classroom. This was the Invisible Genius functioning as an institution builder. He was no longer just an artist. He was a leader who sought to empower the next generation.

His collaborations with Scott Hayden and Arthur Marshall were particularly influential. He co-composed *The Swipesy Cakewalk* with Hayden to help the young man establish a professional reputation. His relationship with Arthur Marshall was even more comprehensive. Joplin helped Marshall secure a job at the Maple Leaf Club. He also ensured that Marshall enrolled in music theory courses.

To Joplin, mentorship was a form of radical politics. By providing professional opportunities and emphasizing education, he was creating a roadmap for Black advancement. He understood that individual success was fragile. True liberation required a community of educated and disciplined creators. The "Sedalia Scene" was not just a collection of musicians. It was a blueprint for an intellectual movement.

CHAPTER 3
THE DOUBLE-EDGED SWORD OF SHOW BUSINESS

In the modern age blackface is unanimously viewed in bad taste as a visceral and symbolic remnant of systemic dehumanisation. It is a legacy that reduced Black identity to a mocking caricature for the amusement of white audiences. This cultural toxicity is so potent that even modern attempts at satire often struggle to escape the weight of history. A primary example is Robert Downey Jr.'s performance in the 2008 film *Tropic Thunder*. While the role was designed to lampoon the ego of method actors rather than the Black community itself, it remains a lightning rod for controversy. Despite receiving an Academy Award nomination at the time, the portrayal has faced significant retrospective backlash. This debate highlights a modern consensus: the historical pain associated with the practice is so deep, that it cannot be easily neutralised by artistic irony.

For Scott Joplin, this was not a theoretical debate but a professional reality. He entered an industry where the only available platform was often one built on his own degradation, forcing him to navigate the double-edged sword of achieving success through a medium that sought to strip him of his dignity. From our modern viewpoint, we see this compromise as a high-stakes gamble. Joplin was trading his cultural capital for the financial resources needed to eventually transcend the very industry that sought to mock him. It was a calculated risk taken by a man who understood that his true work lay far beyond the footlights of the minstrel stage.

Minstrelsy and Stereotypes

In the early 20th century, the entertainment industry relied heavily on minstrelsy as its most lucrative enterprise. These shows, featuring performers in blackface engaging in choreographed tomfoolery, were the cornerstone of mass entertainment and a primary source of revenue for white-owned publishing houses.

Minstrelsy was not merely entertainment. It was a reinforcement of social hierarchy. The Jim Crow and Zip Coon characters were designed to reassure white audiences of their own superiority. For a trained musician like Joplin, performing within these constraints was an exercise in extreme psychological discipline. He had to wear a mask of simplicity while composing with a complexity that his audience could not yet perceive. The coon archetype crudely depicted African-Americans as irrational, sub-human, and devoid of genuine personality or intelligence.

Originally, these roles were played by white actors in greasepaint. However, a shift occurred as Black performers began to enter the professional circuit. Many felt compelled to inhabit these demeaning roles simply to secure work, creating a system where Black artists were forced to participate in their own mockery to survive.

Case Studies in Success and Exploitation
Success in the 1890s was often synonymous with the "Coon Song" craze. These were pieces of sheet music that utilised the most offensive lyrical tropes to ensure high sales. While the broader industry exploited the creative labour of Black musicians by forcing them to sell their work for a flat fee and stripping them of future royalties, John Stark took a radically different path. Unlike his competitors, Stark possessed a rare appreciation for the technical complexity of Joplin's compositions. He famously refused to publish the derogatory "coon" caricatures, opting instead for elegant, Art Nouveau cover designs. This professional respect validated Joplin's status as a serious composer, providing him with a platform of dignity that was systematically denied to his peers.

Ernest Hogan became a prolific and wealthy musician after his hit *"All Coons Look Alike to Me"* sold over a million copies. While the song's title and lyrics infuriated many in the Black community, its massive commercial success ironically opened doors for other Black songwriters to enter the mainstream industry.

Although William H. Krell published the first Ragtime instrumental *(Mississippi Rag)*, he later pivoted to capitalise on the coon song craze. He renamed his work *Piccaninny Rag* and utilised offensive sheet music covers to appeal to the prevailing public appetite.

The influence of these tropes extended to female composers as well. May Aufderheide's best-selling piece, *The Thriller,* utilised blackface imagery and standard coon tropes to ensure its marketability in a crowded field.

Participation and Survival

For Joplin, the minstrel stage was not an end but a tactical means. During the mid-1890s, he toured with minstrel troupes on the "coon" circuit.. These performances required him to inhabit the very caricatures he sought to dismantle. However, beneath the greasepaint, Joplin was conducting a quiet revolution. He used the steady income from these tours to fund his education at George R. Smith College. He was effectively using the earnings to finance his transition into a serious composer.

Today we recognise this as a form of intellectual laundering. He was taking the dirty money of the minstrel circuit and refining it into the pure capital of musical theory. He understood that to be his own master, as Douglass argued, he first had to survive the mastery of others. His participation was a calculated sacrifice of his immediate dignity to secure his long-term agency.

In 1901, Joplin published *I Am Thinking of my Pickaninny Days*. This composition stands as a stark example of his participation in industry trends. It shows that even a genius was forced to make artistic compromises to maintain visibility.

These examples illustrate the reality of the era's racial power dynamics. Success was not a matter of pure merit; it was a navigation of a double-edged sword where career advancement often required a degree of self-abasement.

Professional Rivalries

The Ragtime market of the early 1900s was a battlefield of egos and intellectual property. Joplin was not a passive victim of the industry; he was a fierce competitor. He engaged in cutting contests and professional rivalries to assert his technical superiority. His self-promotion was often tied to his insistence on classical standards. By branding himself as the "King of Ragtime Composers," he was carving out a space that was distinct from the interchangeable coon song writers of Tin Pan Alley.

His rivalry with other performers was often an attempt to police the quality of the genre. He viewed sloppy or fast playing as a reinforcement of the very stereotypes he hated. By demanding a specific, disciplined tempo, he was forcing his audience to listen to the architecture of the music rather than the antics of the performer. This was his most potent tool for self-promotion: the undeniable evidence of his own technical mastery.

Joplin's Invisible Genius stood in sharp contrast to figures like Ben Harney. A white performer who frequently performed in blackface to gain "authentic" credibility, Harney aggressively marketed himself as the "Father of Ragtime." This approach prioritised immediate fame and commercial viability over the sophisticated, enduring art that Joplin sought to create. Harney sought to own the present through marketing, but Joplin worked to own the future through excellence. It was a battle not just for a title, but for the very soul and ownership of the genre.

While Harney's self-proclaimed title won him temporary headlines, his music lacked the structural depth required for longevity. As the Ragtime craze cooled, Harney faded into obscurity. In his later years, he made desperate, failed attempts to reclaim his status, but the musical landscape had moved beyond the shallow novelty of his compositions. Ultimately, history delivered a decisive verdict. Harney's commercial shortcuts ensured his work became a dated relic of the minstrel era, whereas Joplin's refusal to sacrifice artistic integrity for a quick profit ensured that his work survived the collapse of the industry that birthed it. Consequently, Harney is now a footnote in the history of appropriation, while Joplin remains the undisputed architect of the form.

The entertainment culture of the era favoured the creation of pompous personas to cut through the noise of a crowded market. A primary example of this was Jelly Roll Morton, who famously and controversially claimed to be the sole inventor of jazz. Morton represented a segment of the industry that valued aggressive self-promotion and the immediate accumulation of cultural capital above all else. While Morton's theatrics were designed to capture the spotlight of the moment, Joplin's focus remained on the quiet, meticulous documentation of his work. This divergence highlights the tension between the artist as a performer and the artist as an architect.

Joplin found himself at a crossroads with an industry that prioritised the immediate gratification of catchy, comedic hooks over structural complexity. While many performers leaned into the profitable caricatures of the minstrel stage, Joplin chose a path of intellectual sovereignty. He sought to define Ragtime as a high-order discipline, applying the rigour of classical architecture to a genre the market viewed as disposable. By refusing to devalue his work for the sake of populist profit, Joplin was not merely competing for space. He was engineering a new standard of cultural value that demanded the respect of posterity.

Cultural Capital vs. Dehumanisation

While minstrelsy was immensely denigrating, it paradoxically provided the financial foundation and the global platform necessary for Black musicians to launch their careers. It was a predatory gateway that nevertheless preserved the rhythmic seeds of modern American music.

Late in his life, Ernest Hogan expressed deep shame and regret for his role in the "coon song" era. However, he also credited the genre for the preservation of Ragtime, highlighting the tragic trade-off required of Black artists in that period.

The era of "coon songs" remains a lasting testament

to the systemic denigration of African Americans in the post-slavery era, serving as a reminder of the steep price performers often paid for the right to be heard. Yet, Joplin's victory is found in the endurance of his scores.

While the offensive lyrics of his contemporaries have been relegated to the archives of shame, Joplin's melodies remain vibrant. He proved that excellence is a universal solvent. By pouring his genius into the formal structures of the piano rag and the opera, he created a body of work that eventually outlived the caricatures. His legacy is a testament to the idea that while a system may seek to strip a man of his dignity, a master can always rebuild it through the permanence of his art.

CHAPTER 4

THE INTELLECTUAL BATTLEGROUND

The music of Scott Joplin was not a detached artistic endeavour; rather, it was a rhythmic manifestation of the most significant intellectual struggle in Black American history. While the "King of Ragtime" was perfecting the syncopation of his masterpieces, the foundational architects of Black thought were engaged in a fierce war of ideas regarding the path to true liberation. Joplin's work reveals a composer deeply aligned with the pragmatic conservatism of the era, a philosophy that prioritized the building of internal power over the performance of external protest.

By anchoring his Invisible Genius in the self-reliance and economic grit championed by Booker T. Washington, Joplin offered a compelling answer to the systemic oppression of the South. He proved that the most radical act an individual can perform is to become undeniable through their work. This vision remains a powerful challenge to contemporary activists, suggesting that the pursuit of excellence and the mastery of high-order culture are the most effective weapons in the struggle for dignity and agency.

The Strategic Crossroads
History occasionally delights in synchronicity. The

year 1868 saw the birth of both Scott Joplin and W.E.B. Du Bois. These two men, born into the same dawn of Reconstruction, would eventually personify two divergent paths for Black advancement. While Du Bois would ascend to lead the charge for political agitation, Joplin's career more closely mirrored a different, more grounded blueprint.

As a pragmatic conservative, Booker T. Washington (born 1856) became the era's most influential figure by advocating for "industrial education" and entrepreneurship. He believed that economic independence and professional discipline were the primary shields against the volatility of a hostile society.

While Scott Joplin's career was anchored in Washingtonian pragmatism, he was simultaneously a living embodiment of the "Talented Tenth", the concept popularized by W.E.B. Du Bois in his 1903 essay. Du Bois argued that the African-American community would be saved by its exceptional men: the intellectual elite who, through higher education and classical training, would lead the masses away from the "contamination and death of the Worst."

For Du Bois, the pursuit of industrial education alone was a trap. He believed that if Black

Americans focused solely on becoming better carpenters or blacksmiths, they would remain a permanent underclass, denied the "bread of life" found in the liberal arts. He demanded a leadership class that could master the "best of human thought" to challenge the moral and intellectual foundations of white supremacy. Joplin, with his mastery of complex harmony and his insistence on the formal opera, was precisely the kind of "exceptional man" Du Bois envisioned.

However, the tragedy of the Invisible Genius lay in the friction between these two strategies. Joplin was a "Talented Tenth" mind operating in a "Washingtonian" marketplace. He possessed the high-order culture Du Bois championed, yet he lacked the political and social infrastructure to support it. While the elite Black intelligentsia often looked down on Ragtime as low brow or vulgar music, Joplin was busy elevating it to the level of the German masters. He was a man caught between worlds: too sophisticated for the minstrel stage, yet too syncopated for the rigid classical establishment.

This section of Joplin's life reveals the limitations of both ideologies. Excellence, as Joplin discovered, was not a magic key that immediately opened the doors of the Metropolitan Opera. His struggle proved that while the "Talented Tenth" could achieve intellectual sovereignty, they still had to navigate the brutal economic realities of a society that valued Black labour but feared Black genius. From our vantage point in 2017, we see that Joplin's true victory was in refusing to choose. He used the pragmatic tools of the entrepreneur to fund the "Talented Tenth" dreams of the composer.

The Atlanta Compromise and Plessy v. Ferguson
The world in which Scott Joplin operated was not merely a cultural landscape; it was a minefield of shifting legalities and survivalist bargains. In 1895, Booker T. Washington stood before the Cotton States and International Exposition and proposed what became known as the "Atlanta Compromise." This was a tactical trade of staggering proportions: Black Americans would temporarily submit to white political rule and social segregation in exchange for the right to basic education and economic due process. It was a strategy of quiet accumulation by devising a plan to build a fortress of internal power while the storm of Jim Crow raged outside.

However, the legal architecture of the era was moving faster than Washington's bargain. Only a year later, the 1896 *Plessy v. Ferguson* judgment crystallised the "separate but equal" doctrine into the law of the land. This ruling did more than just mandate segregated railway cars; it reinforced a curriculum that sought to limit Black education to the narrowest possible vocational and industrial training. The state's vision for the Black mind was one of utility, not artistry. It was a world of hammers and ploughs, deliberately designed to exclude the classical and liberal arts education that Joplin so fervently pursued.

Yet, where others saw a conflict between the industrial and the intellectual, Joplin saw a profound synthesis. He did not view his mastery of the piano as a flight from reality, but as the ultimate form of industrial discipline. To Joplin, the rigorous architecture of a fugue or the precise mechanics of a syncopated rag required as much technical grit as any trade. He effectively industrialised his genius. By treating the keyboard as his workbench and the score as his blueprint, he navigated the cost of the Atlanta Compromise without surrendering his soul to its limitations.

Joplin's Musical Intervention
Scott Joplin's intervention in the intellectual war of his era was as rhythmic as it was profound. He utilised the very liberal arts that Du Bois cherished to achieve with the economic independence that Washington demanded. By applying the rigorous structures of European classical music to the African-American pulse of Ragtime, he created a

synthesis that transcended both camps. He was proving that the Black mind was capable of high-order complexity, even while operating within a commercial market that sought to keep it industrial and subservient.

This political alignment was made explicit through his choice of subjects. His 1903 opera, *A Guest of Honor*, was written specifically to commemorate the 1901 dinner between President Theodore Roosevelt and Booker T. Washington at the White House. This was a bold musical endorsement of Washington's leadership and a celebration of Black entry into the highest seats of American power. Joplin was not just writing music; he was documenting a shift in the national landscape.

The connection to the Roosevelt administration continued with his 1902 rag, *The Strenuous Life*, named directly after one of the President's most famous speeches on the virtues of hard work and grit. Through these works, Joplin positioned himself as a composer of the Washington Era. He utilised his art to bridge the gap between Black intellectual leadership and the American presidency, suggesting that excellence was the most effective diplomatic tool available to his race.

Ultimately, Joplin viewed high art as the ultimate

form of politics. By choosing the demanding medium of grand opera for *Treemonisha,* he asserted that African Americans had a fundamental right to excel in the most sophisticated traditions of the Western world. Every meticulously placed note was a strike against the shroud of obscurity. He refused to be a mere folk musician or a minstrel caricature. Instead, he positioned himself as a formal architect of sound, using the quietest of weapons, the ink on a score, to declare a state of intellectual independence that no legal ruling could touch.

The Defence of Creative Freedom

The debate surrounding the path to Black advancement was not without its internal friction. Popular criticisms of the era, often led by the Niagara Movement, accused Booker T. Washington of prophesying a surrender of civil rights. These critics argued that focusing solely on vocational skills would inadvertently create a permanent class of labourers, forever subservient to the white industrial machine. They feared that by trading political agitation for economic process, the race would lose its soul to the factory floor.

However, Scott Joplin's career highlights the overlooked strength of this less militant, meritocratic path. By mastering a field as complex and intellectually demanding as classical music, he exposed the absurdity of segregation more effectively than a protest alone could. He was a living contradiction to the logic of *Plessy v. Ferguson.* If a man could architect the sophisticated harmonies of a concert waltz or a grand opera, the argument for his inherent inferiority collapsed under the weight of his own excellence.

In this light, Joplin reinterpreted the Washingtonian focus on thrift and grit. He did not view these as ends in themselves, but as the scaffolding for the human spirit. He believed that the spirit, fired by creativity and an openness to knowledge, provided the ultimate motivation for liberation. His pursuit of creative freedom was the final stage of his human capital strategy. Having built his economic foundation through the Ragtime markets, he used that independence to defend his right to experiment, to fail, and ultimately to define his own masterpiece.

Modern Echoes of Joplin's Timeless Message

The strategies of Washington and Du Bois continue to find a vibrant home in the twenty-first century. Movements such as *#BlackLivesMatter* represent a necessary evolution of the Du Boisian tradition. They focus on systemic agitation and the demand for collective visibility. Their insistence on institutional reform is a justified response to enduring structural inequities. However, this outward-facing approach has inherent limitations. It often prioritises the dismantling of external barriers over the cultivation of the internal human capital that Joplin so meticulously engineered. By focusing primarily on the external structures that restrict life, these movements risk neglecting the sovereign development required to lead within a reformed world. This strategic gap highlights the need for a more pragmatic, internally-focused framework.

The work of contemporary thinkers such as Thomas Sowell and Walter Williams provides a modern framework for contextualising Joplin's success. As Sowell notes in Basic Economics: "The most important of all resources is human capital. This is the knowledge and the skills in people's heads."[1] Sowell's observation offers a definitive lens through which to analyse Joplin's early development. The rigorous instruction provided by Julius Weiss represented the strategic accumulation of human capital - an asset that proved vital in a segregated society. By mastering a technical discipline that was universally recognised, Joplin secured a market position that transcended regional prejudice and social barriers.

---

[1] Sowell, Thomas. *Basic Economics: A Common Sense Guide to the Economy.* 4th ed. New York: Basic Books, 2010.

Walter Williams famously argued that "the beautiful thing about the market is that it is the most effective weapon against racism. The market rewards excellence regardless of the background of the worker."[2] The commercial triumph of *The Maple Leaf Rag* serves as a historical testament to this principle. The music permeated white households not through political appeal, but through the sheer superiority of its craft. The market's inherent focus on quality forced a prioritization of merit over prejudice. This allowed Joplin's genius to transcend the rigid racial barriers of the era.

The Joplin narrative offers a complementary perspective that remains equally vital. It suggests that while the struggle for systemic change is necessary, it is most effectively sustained by the quiet, internal accumulation of human capital. Joplin's life was an argument for the power of self-reliance. He believed that the mastery of a discipline provided a form of security that no political shift could fully guarantee.

Today these two paths are the twin engines of advancement. The radical intellectual demands change, while the pragmatic conservative ensures the individual is prepared to lead when that shift

---

[2] Williams, Walter E. *The State Against Blacks*. New York: McGraw-Hill, 1982.

occurs. Joplin's genius was his focus on craft amidst turmoil. He proved that excellence is a silent protest that eventually speaks louder than any slogan. True liberation is found at the intersection of external justice and internal mastery.

CHAPTER 5

TREEMONISHA: A VISION OF LITERACY

If the *Maple Leaf Rag* served as the foundational bedrock of Scott Joplin's commercial career, then *Treemonisha* was its ultimate, elevated purpose. The three-act opera was far more than a musical composition; it was a deliberate political manifesto that championed education as the singular, non-negotiable tool for liberation. In an era of profound social and legal restriction, Joplin utilised the operatic stage, essentially the highest altitude of Western cultural expression, to present a radical argument: the greatest threat to a community was not external force, but the internal rot of ignorance.

Much of what we understand today about the creation, the struggle, and the near-obliteration of this masterpiece is owed to the meticulous detective work of Edward A. Berlin. As the pre-eminent Joplin scholar and biographer, Berlin's research in King of Ragtime provides the essential scaffolding for our modern appreciation of the opera. It is through his exhaustive archival recovery that we see Joplin not just as a songwriter, but as a dramatist of the Human Capital theory.

Treemonisha represents the final, most sophisticated manifestation of the Invisible Genius. It took the pragmatic virtues of self-reliance and literacy, the very core of the Washingtonian strategy, and transformed them into a soaring work of high art. To Joplin, and as Berlin's research suggests, the opera was his "last will and testament"[3] to his people. It remains a timeless testament to the belief that knowledge is the only currency that can truly purchase a permanent freedom.

The Plot: Literacy vs. Superstition

The narrative of *Treemonisha* is a stark allegorical battle between the light of education and the shadows of superstition. Set on a plantation in Arkansas, the opera follows a young woman, *Treemonisha,* who is the only member of her community blessed with the ability to read. She finds herself in direct conflict with a group of conjurers who maintain their power by exploiting the fears and illiteracy of the people. This is not merely a folk tale; it is a dramatisation of the struggle for intellectual sovereignty.

Joplin's protagonist is the quintessential "Talented Tenth" leader. She does not lead through physical might or political agitation, but through the authority of the written word. Edward Berlin notes that Joplin's obsession with this theme likely

---

[3] For the definitive account of Joplin's transition from ragtime to grand opera and the systemic barriers he faced during the composition of *Treemonisha*, see Edward A. Berlin, *King of Ragtime: Scott Joplin and His Era* (1994)

mirrored his own life-long pursuit of formal education. He believed that the shroud of obscurity could only be pierced by the sharp edge of a disciplined mind. By placing a literate woman at the centre of his work, Joplin was arguing that the future of the race depended on the intellectual elevation of its most capable individuals.

A Personal Geography
The setting of the opera, near Texarkana, on the border of Texas and Arkansas is a deeply personal geography. This was the landscape of Joplin's youth, a place where he first witnessed the transformative power of the piano and the stifling weight of the post-Reconstruction South. Berlin's biographical work tracks how Joplin's return to these roots in his writing was an act of cultural reclamation.

By setting his grand opera in the red mud of his childhood, Joplin was asserting that the most sophisticated art forms in the world could grow from the very soil that systemic prejudice sought to keep barren. This act connected his childhood roots to his mature intellectual ambitions. He was taking the raw materials of his own experience and refining them through the fires of classical theory, proving that the American South was capable of producing more than just labour, it could produce genius.

Artistic Ambition: Beyond Ragtime

Joplin insisted that *Treemonisha* was a grand opera. He rejected the idea that it was merely an extension of Ragtime. While he used African-American musical styles, he utilised the structures of European traditions. Although the public and his publishers clamoured for more syncopated piano miniatures, Joplin was looking further out toward the horizon of Wagner and Verdi.

Joplin was proving that a Black composer could master the most complex artistic forms of the Western world. Historians call the opera a "celebration of literacy." It provided a remarkably early voice for civil rights. It showed that community solidarity was built through shared intellectual excellence. For the Invisible Genius, the opera house was the ultimate battlefield for dignity.

The Tragedy of the 1915 Read-Through

The historical record of *Treemonisha* is punctuated by one of the most heart-breaking moments in American music. In 1915, at a rehearsal hall in Harlem, Joplin attempted a read-through of the opera. Lacking the funds for an orchestra or a full production, he sat at the piano himself to provide the accompaniment.

Berlin describes this event as a devastating turning

point. Without the lush orchestration Joplin had envisioned, the naked piano score failed to capture the imagination of the few investors and critics in attendance. The invisible genius was, in that moment, tragically literal. The audience saw a man struggling at a piano, his coordination already beginning to fail him, but they could not hear the symphony playing in his head. This failure accelerated Joplin's physical and mental decline, marking the beginning of the end for the master.

The poor reception left the work shrouded in obscurity for sixty years. But this failure was not a reflection of the musical quality. Instead, it highlighted the severe lack of capital and resources available to Black artists attempting to stage high art in the early twentieth century. Joplin's vision was simply too large for the economic constraints of his era. This performance serves as a tragic bookend to his life.

A Triumph of Hope
Despite the silence that followed the 1915 rehearsal, the legacy of *Treemonisha* is ultimately a triumph of hope over experience. Joplin's self-publication of the score in 1911 ensured that his vision was preserved, even if it could not be performed in his lifetime. He had successfully documented his human capital, leaving behind a blueprint for future generations to

discover.

Fully realising the Joplin legacy requires a modern and grand staging of the opera. Despite the landmark 1975 premiere at the Metropolitan Opera, many believe this vision remains unfinished. The conductor and pianist William Appling famously pursued a version of the work that matched the full scale of Joplin's original ambition until his death, viewing a truly grand staging as the final piece of the Joplin jigsaw. While several productions have emerged since the 1970s, the intricate details of that landmark transformative restaging are explored in depth later in Chapter 7.

CHAPTER 6
THE MYSTERY OF THE MISSING
MANUSCRIPTS

The story of Scott Joplin does not end with a final, triumphant flourish; it dissolves into a silence that is both physical and historical. The final years of the Invisible Genius were defined by a cruel, systemic irony. The man who had gifted America its most vibrant, syncopated pulse eventually lost the coordination of his own hands to the ravages of neurosyphilis. Yet, the tragedy of his decline was only the beginning. The shroud of obscurity that Joplin feared did not lift upon his death in 1917. Instead, it was stitched shut by a series of legal mishaps, institutional indifference, and the cold bureaucracy of debt.

To study Joplin today is to engage in an act of mourning for what remains absent. We are forced to reckon with the staggering reality that entire symphonies, piano concertos, and grand operas (the very summits of his intellectual ambition) vanished into the void of lost history. These were not merely songs; they were the pillars of his Human Capital, the evidence of a Black creator working at the absolute frontier of Western classical form.

This chapter explores how the blunt machinery of the probate court and the chaotic transition of personal estates allowed a master's life's work to be treated as discardable property. From the confiscated trunks of a failed tour in Kansas to the lost archives of the Sweatman estate, Joplin's legacy remains a jigsaw puzzle where the most complex and revelatory patterns are still waiting to be found. The silence of these missing manuscripts is not just a musical loss; it is a hollow space in the American story that continues to haunt the archives a century later.

The Final Movement: Illness and Death
The final movement of Scott Joplin's life was not a grand finale but a slow and discordant fade into a specific kind of darkness. It was a descent that the society of 1917 preferred to keep hidden behind a veil of silence. At that time, syphilis was far more than a medical condition. It was a profound moral stigma that carried a heavy weight of public judgement.

In the moral landscape of the Progressive Era, syphilis was explicitly linked to what reformers called the "Social Evil." This term was a polite euphemism for prostitution. To contract the disease was viewed as a visible confession of a visit to a brothel or a life of illicit wandering. Public health officials and religious leaders framed the infection as a biological consequence of "degeneracy." They believed it was a physical manifestation of a lack of self-control and a failure of character.

This link to degeneracy was weaponised with particular cruelty against the Black community and the world of itinerant musicians. Critics of the era often associated Ragtime music with low brow environments like saloons and gambling halls. Consequently, Joplin's illness was not seen as a private tragedy. It was viewed by many as a predictable outcome for a man operating in such seemingly unrefined social circles. The disease was considered a symbolic marker of a moral crisis rather than a failure of public health. Sufferers were often viewed as outcasts who were unlikely to be welcomed into a respectable home.

The disease is often called "the great imitator" because its symptoms can mask themselves for decades. It moves from a simple initial infection to a systemic invasion that finally targets the central nervous system. This terminal stage is known as neurosyphilis. It causes chronic inflammation that leads the brain tissue itself to break down. For a man whose entire existence was built on the precision of a syncopated beat, the physical loss of motor control was a particular cruelty.

Joplin began to suffer from a total loss of dexterity

and coordination known as ataxia. His fingers slowly lost the ability to navigate the complex keys of the instrument he had mastered. By 1916, the infection had already begun to riddle his brain. He was forced to watch his own talent vanish. He remained conscious of the genius he had once possessed but found himself unable to execute the simplest melody.

The tragedy of this decline is deepened by the fact that a simple cure was less than three decades away. While an earlier arsenic-based treatment called Salvarsan appeared in 1910, it was often too toxic and too late for those already in advanced stages. The miracle of Penicillin would not be discovered until 1928, and did not become available to the general public until the mid-1940s, which was roughly thirty years after Joplin was laid to rest.

His final months were spent within the walls of the Manhattan State Hospital on Ward's Island. He was admitted to the mental institution in February 1917 as the dementia took its final hold. He died there on 1 April 1917 at the age of forty-nine. The "King of Ragtime" passed away disturbed and penniless. He was buried in an unmarked pauper's grave at Saint Michaels Cemetery in New York. He remained anonymous in that earth for fifty-seven years. It took the cultural revival of the 1970s for the world to finally mark the spot where its most influential composer lay in wait for his recognition.

The Executor: Wilbur "Sensational" Sweatman

If Scott Joplin was the quiet and cerebral architect of ragtime, then Wilbur Sweatman was its vibrant and high-voltage messenger. Known to the vaudeville circuits as "Sensational" Sweatman, he was a man of immense theatrical flair. He famously dazzled audiences by playing three clarinets simultaneously. This created a wall of sound that bridged the gap between the structured world of ragtime and the emerging wildness of jazz. Their friendship was not merely a professional association. It was a bond forged in the soil of Missouri and tempered in the frantic energy of New York. Sweatman had been a champion of Joplin's work since the beginning. He was responsible for the earliest known recording of *The Maple Leaf Rag* on a phonograph cylinder in 1903. Although no copies of that recording survive today, it represents a ghost of their early synergy.

By the time Joplin's health began to fail in New York, Sweatman had become an essential pillar of support. He did not just manage the composer's business affairs. He became a fixture in the Joplin household. He lived for a time in the boarding house operated by Joplin's widow, Lottie, on 131st

Street in Harlem. In that house, Sweatman acted as a sentinel for the Invisible Genius. Lottie trusted him implicitly. She saw him as a man who understood the weight of her husband's legacy. When Joplin drafted his final wishes, naming Sweatman as the executor was a move of profound trust. It was an attempt to place his life's work in the hands of a man who was already a star in the new world of jazz.

Sweatman's own career was a testament to the Human Capital theory later championed by Thomas Sowell. He was the first African-American musician to be offered a long-term recording contract. He navigated the white-dominated vaudeville circuits with a combination of technical mastery and sheer showmanship. His bands became a fertile breeding ground for the next generation of genius. He mentored legends like Duke Ellington and Coleman Hawkins. Yet, despite his own fame, he never allowed the Joplin manuscripts to fall into neglect. For over forty years, he guarded the papers with the devotion of a monk. He generously opened the archives to the few researchers who cared enough to ask.

The tragedy of Sweatman's role as executor lies in the transition of eras. He was a bridge between the "Classical Ragtime" of the 1890s and the "Swing" of the 1940s. He held the keys to a forgotten kingdom. While the world outside was moving toward the bebop of the future, Sweatman sat in Harlem with a trunk full of the past. He remained the primary guardian of Joplin's later creative thoughts until his own death in 1961. He was the only person who knew the full extent of what had been lost. His life was a long and (indeed) sensational vigil for a friend whose music had once predicted the very world Sweatman came to dominate.

The Legal Battle for the Sweatman Estate

The year 1961 marked a catastrophic turning point for American musicology. When Wilbur Sweatman passed away, the sentinel of the Joplin archives was gone. He left behind a void that was both emotional and administrative. In a tragic oversight that would have horrified the meticulous Scott Joplin, Sweatman died intestate. He left no will to govern the distribution of his substantial estate. This failure of formal structure invited a chaos that eventually swallowed the Invisible Genius whole. It was a stark reminder that without the protective scaffolding of the law, even the most significant cultural capital can evaporate in an instant.

A bitter legal battle soon erupted over the Sweatman legacy. At the centre of the storm was his daughter, Barbara. She stood to inherit the estate, but her claim was immediately challenged by other family members. The dispute was rooted in the lingering moral rigidities of an earlier era. They questioned her legitimacy because she had been born out of wedlock. This legal strategy was a cruel echo of the very "Social Evil" stigmas that had haunted Joplin's own reputation. The courtroom became a theatre of internal discord. The pursuit of individual shares of wealth began to take precedence over the preservation of a collective history.

During these prolonged and messy hearings, the unthinkable happened. The massive collection of Joplin's personal papers and unpublished manuscripts simply vanished. While the lawyers argued over birth certificates and lineage, the physical evidence of Joplin's late-period genius was lost to the world. It is a mystery that continues to haunt researchers. Some believe the papers were discarded by indifferent executors. Others suspect they were stolen during the confusion of the probate process. Regardless of the cause, the result was a total blackout of Joplin's final creative thoughts.

The Joplin manuscripts were a form of high-value human capital. They were a gift intended for the future. Yet, because of a lack of legal foresight and the friction of internal family politics, that capital was liquidated. The shroud of obscurity was no longer a result of racial prejudice alone. It was now a consequence of the fragility of a legacy that lacked a formal will to defend it. The silence of the missing papers remains a testament to the fact that excellence must be guarded by order if it is to survive the passage of time.

The Lost Opera: A Guest of Honor

If *Treemonisha* was a vision of the future, then *A Guest of Honor* was Scott Joplin's boldest engagement with the present. Composed in 1903, the opera was not merely a musical suite. It was a high-stakes intellectual monument. Joplin wrote the work to commemorate one of the most controversial events of the Progressive Era. In 1901, President Theodore Roosevelt had invited Booker T. Washington to dine at the White House. This event was a flashpoint that ignited the fury of the segregated South. For Joplin, however, it was a moment of supreme validation. By choosing this subject for a grand opera, he was weaving Washington's pragmatic conservative triumphs into the very fabric of American high culture.

To bring this vision to life, Joplin did not settle for a small-scale production. He founded the Ragtime Opera Company and assembled a formidable troupe of thirty performers. This was a massive undertaking that required significant financial and human capital. It was a manifestation of the "strenuous life" that Roosevelt himself championed. Joplin took his company on a national tour across the Midwest. He hoped to prove that his genius could sustain a full-length dramatic narrative on the professional stage. This was his attempt to move beyond the short-lived fame of the dance hall and into the permanent halls of history.

The tragedy that unfolded in Pittsburg, Kansas, remains one of the most painful episodes in the annals of American music. During a stop on the tour, the company was robbed of its entire box office takings. The theft left Joplin financially destitute and unable to settle the theatre's mounting bills. In a cold and bureaucratic act of confiscation, the theatre management seized the company's trunks and equipment. Inside those trunks lay the only orchestrated score for *A Guest of Honor*. Because Joplin lacked the resources to pay his debts, his personal property remained in legal limbo.

The score was never retrieved. It is believed that the manuscript was eventually discarded or destroyed by people who had no understanding of its historical value. This was more than a financial disaster. It was a systemic erasure of a major intellectual achievement. Because no other copies existed, an entire chapter of Joplin's creative evolution was deleted. The loss of *A Guest of Honor* represents a missing bridge between his early rags and his final masterpiece. It serves as a haunting reminder of how easily the brilliance of the marginalized can be extinguished by the blunt machinery of debt and indifference. The silence of this lost opera is a hollow space in the American canon that no amount of research has yet been able to fill.

The Missing Jigsaw Puzzle
The legacy of Scott Joplin is a house with many of its structural beams removed. There is an extraordinary and bitter prescience in his famous remark that he would finally be recognised twenty-five years after his death. He understood that he was writing for a future that had not yet arrived. Yet, he could not have foreseen that the very future he predicted would be forced to work with a fragmented canon. The Invisible Genius remains partially invisible not by choice, but by the chaotic intervention of fate. We are left to reconstruct the mind of a master using only the shards that survived the fire of poverty and the flood of legal negligence.

The list of what is missing is a catalogue of unrealised potential. We know of a *Symphony No. 1* and a *Piano Concerto*, works that would have definitively moved the needle of Black contribution to the Western classical tradition. There is also the mysterious *Mayflower Rag*. This lost work represents a significant historical grievance. Joplin allegedly believed that the white songwriter Irving Berlin had plagiarised the Mayflower to create the global sensation *Alexander's Ragtime Band*. Without the manuscript, this remains a haunting "what if" of music history. It is a specific instance where the lack of documented human capital allowed the cultural credit, and the massive royalties to flow away from the creator and into the pockets of the establishment.

When the physical evidence of a person's intellect is lost, they are robbed of their place in the meritocratic hierarchy. The search for these manuscripts is therefore more than a sentimental journey for musicologists. It is a necessary act of historical restoration. It is an attempt to recover the "wealth" of a mind that was systematically undervalued during its time.

These missing pieces are a call to action. Every lost note remains a lost argument for the depth of the Black intellectual tradition. Until these manuscripts are recovered, the Invisible Genius remains a king without his full regalia. Their silence is a hollow space in the story of American progress.

CHAPTER 7
THE CENTENNIAL RESURRECTION

The 1970s did not merely bring a revival of Scott Joplin's music. They witnessed a total resurrection of his intellectual stature. For over fifty years, his name had been relegated to the footnotes of American music, often dismissed as a composer of "quaint" or "honky-tonk" novelties. The silence that followed his death was finally shattered by a generation that was ready to listen to ragtime as he had intended: as a formal, classical discipline. This era saw the Invisible Genius step out from the shadows of history and onto the world's most prestigious stages. It was the moment the jigsaw puzzle began to find its most vital pieces. It was also the moment that the responsibility for his legacy shifted from the archives of the past to the collective efforts of the present.

Joshua Rifkin: The Turning Point
The spark for this revolution was as quiet as it was profound. In 1970, a young musicologist and pianist named Joshua Rifkin released an album that would fundamentally alter the American musical landscape: *Scott Joplin: Piano Rags*. This was not merely a collection of songs; it was a manifesto. Rifkin stripped away the frantic, "honky-tonk" speed that had plagued Joplin's reputation for decades. He played the scores with a deliberate,

scholarly reverence, adhering to Joplin's own printed warning: "It is never right to play Ragtime fast."

The public response was seismic. The album earned a Grammy nomination and signalled a permanent shift in perception. Ragtime was no longer viewed as trivial background music for a dusty saloon. It was recognised, perhaps for the first time by a mass audience, as a coherent and sophisticated body of work. Rifkin treated the *Maple Leaf Rag* and *Gladiolus Rag* with the same technical precision one might afford a Chopin nocturne. This approach proved that there was a massive, untapped market for Black excellence in its most disciplined form.

A poignant case study in this revival is the redemption of *The Ragtime Dance*. When it was first published in 1902, the piece was deemed a "commercial disappointment." Joplin's publisher, John Stark, had been deeply unconvinced by the work's complexity and its length, which included vocal cues and dance instructions. He had initially refused to publish it, doubting its marketability. However, seventy years after its debut, Rifkin's version of the piece sold over one million copies. It finally found the sophisticated market Joplin had envisioned during the heights of the Sedalia scene, a market that recognised the piece not as a simple novelty, but as a masterclass in syncopated structure.

This elevation of prestige was further solidified by Gunther Schuller and the New England Ragtime Ensemble. In 1973, their recording of *Scott Joplin: The Red Back Book* achieved what many in the ragtime era would have thought impossible. It won a Grammy for Best Chamber Music Performance. By placing Joplin's arrangements alongside the canon of high-order chamber music, Schuller and Rifkin proved that the Invisible Genius had always belonged in the conservatory. The 1970s did not just popularise Joplin; they canonised him.

The Sting and the Global Renaissance
If Joshua Rifkin provided the intellectual foundation for the revival, then the 1973 film *The Sting* provided the global megaphone. Director George Roy Hill made the inspired, albeit anachronistic, decision to score a film set in the 1930s with Joplin's turn-of-the-century rags. This creative choice by Hill and adapter Marvin Hamlisch ignited a cultural wildfire. The film became a juggernaut of the era, securing ten Academy Award nominations and winning seven, including Best Picture and Best Music (Original Song Score or Adaptation).

This level of institutional recognition ensured that

Joplin's music reached a vast global audience, transcending the borders of both race and geography. The film's theme, *The Entertainer,* became more than just a "Joplin tune." It evolved into one of the most iconic pieces of music in history, often cited alongside the works of Beethoven or Mozart in its instant recognisability. In 1974, it reached number three on the Billboard Hot 100, a feat that validated Joplin's lifelong belief that his music was not a fleeting fad, but a permanent contribution to the global soundscape.

The impact of this pop-culture explosion had a profound physical consequence. As the world hummed the melodies of the Invisible Genius, the silence surrounding his final resting place became a matter of public shame. This 1970s revival provided the necessary momentum to address the tragedy of Joplin's unceremonious funeral that saw his body laid in an unmarked pauper's grave.

Spurred by the newfound prestige of the Pulitzer-recognised composer, a collective of fans, historians, and activists finally took action. In 1974, the same year *The Entertainer* was dominating the charts, a bronze marker was finally placed over his grave. It was a symbolic unearthing. For fifty-seven years, the earth had kept him anonymous, but the cultural tide of the 1970s was too strong to ignore. The man who had been buried "disturbed and penniless" was now being treated as a national treasure. The marker served as a physical confession that society was finally ready to acknowledge the genius it had once allowed to fade into the New York soil.

The Pulitzer Prize: An Establishment Apology
The peak of this centennial resurrection occurred in 1976, during the American Bicentennial. In a move that felt like a formal reconciliation with history, the Pulitzer Prize Committee awarded Scott Joplin a posthumous Special Citation. The award officially recognised his contributions to the American musical canon and his role as the architect of a unique national sound. This was more than a mere trophy; it was a profound establishment apology. For decades, the intellectual gatekeepers of American culture had dismissed his work as transient novelty. The Pulitzer Citation effectively ended that era of condescension, confirming that the Invisible Genius had finally been seen by the highest authorities in the land.

This year of national celebration brought other tangible acts of restoration. In Missouri, the state where the "Sedalia Scene" had first hummed to life - Joplin's former residence at 2658-A Delmar Boulevard in St. Louis was added to the National Register of Historic Places. The house where Joplin lived when he composed *The Entertainer* was designated as a National Historic Landmark. This was a crucial development in the Human Capital narrative. By preserving the physical space where his intellect had laboured, the government was acknowledging that the geography of Black genius was as worthy of protection as the homes of presidents or generals.

The momentum of the decade even reached the cinematic world of biographical representation. In 1977, the film *Scott Joplin* was released, starring Billy Dee Williams in the title role. While the film took significant creative liberties and was heavily entertainment-driven, its impact was undeniable. It served as a visual testament to his struggle, bringing the tragic narrative of his final years to a television and cinema audience. Even when the script traded historical precision for drama, the film helped keep Joplin's legacy in the public eye during the closing years of the decade.

Together, these events represented a systematic rebuilding of a legacy that had been nearly erased. From the halls of the Pulitzer committee to the brick-and-mortar preservation of his St. Louis home, the mid-1970s functioned as a collective cultural effort to right a historical wrong. The Invisible Genius was no longer just a name on a piece of sheet music; he was a recognised landmark of the American experience. This period ensured that Joplin's voice would not just be heard, but that his life would be anchored in the official records of the nation he had helped define.

Treemonisha at the Met: The Vision Realised

The most profound validation of the 1970s revival took place on the operatic stage. For decades, *Treemonisha* had been a ghost, a legendary lost work known only to a handful of scholars through its vocal score. The silence first began to break in 1972 with a notable premiere in Atlanta. Although it was a modest production, it served as the essential spark for the fire that followed.

That momentum reached a crescendo in 1975 when the Houston Grand Opera mounted a lavish, professional production. This staging was the true precursor to the work's final ascent. Under the direction of Frank Corsaro and featuring the choreography of Katherine Dunham, the opera finally received the grand treatment Joplin had died trying to secure. When this production eventually moved to the Metropolitan Opera in New York later that year, it became a historic milestone. This was the moment the invisible genius was finally permitted to speak in the language he cherished most: the language of grand opera.

The journey of the production became a revelation in itself. It travelled from Houston to the Palace Theatre on Broadway before arriving at the hallowed stage of the Metropolitan Opera House. Witnessing the work performed by a world-class cast with a full orchestra dismantled the 1915 criticism that Joplin's ambitions were a delusion of grandeur. The performance revealed a coherent and visionary drama rather than a mere collection of ragtime tunes stitched together. This staging proved that Joplin had successfully synthesised the African-American experience with the formal structures of European Romanticism.

The timing of this resurrection was critical. Performed in the wake of the Civil Rights Movement, the opera's central themes; the struggle for literacy, the rejection of superstition, and the election of a female leader, all resonated with a modern audience in ways that Joplin's contemporaries could never have grasped. The celebration of literacy at the heart of the plot was no longer just a Victorian ideal; it was a living political statement.

By the time the curtain fell at the Met, the Invisible Genius had been fully vindicated. The production turned *Treemonisha* from a tragic footnote into a living masterpiece. It provided the final, undeniable proof that Joplin's intellect was not limited to the short-form genius of the piano rag. He was a master of large-scale architecture. The achievement at the Met served as the ultimate restoration of his dignity. It confirmed that his vision was not a failure of talent, but a casualty of a society that was simply not yet ready to listen.

The Modern Mandate: Assembling the Jigsaw
The 1970s transformed Scott Joplin from a historical curiosity into a permanent pillar of the American canon. While the public enjoyed film scores, scholars engaged in a massive undertaking of historical recovery. This was the moment the Invisible Genius was finally seen in his full, complex totality.

A landmark in this effort was the work of Richard "Dick" Zimmerman. In 1974, he released a monumental five-LP collection, *Scott Joplin: His Complete Works*. This was the first modern attempt to document the entire surviving canon in a single, authoritative set. Zimmerman's project served as a physical manifesto for the composer's legacy. It provided a definitive library for a new generation of listeners and scholars. By gathering these fragmented pieces, he ensured that Joplin's genius could never again be dismissed as a series of isolated novelties.

This cumulative effort represented the fulfilment of Joplin's own extraordinary prescience. During his final years, Joplin expressed a quiet trust that future generations would recognise his talent. He understood he was composing for a world that did not yet exist. The 1970s marked the arrival of that world. The restoration of his home and the recognition of his music were the overdue response to a strategist who waited for the world to catch up.

CHAPTER 8
FROM VICE TO VIRTUE: A LINGERING
LEGACY

The connection between Scott Joplin and the genres that followed ragtime is not merely a matter of rhythm. It is an evolution that can be mapped as a foundational code for American music. While the 1970s revival restored Joplin to the classical stage, his most enduring impact is found in the way his successors navigated the precarious waters of American vice. Joplin provided the first blueprint for the artist as a Trojan horse; a creator who could smuggle sophisticated intellectual property into the heart of a culture that initially viewed their work as a contagion.

Joplin provided the blueprint for how a Black creator could engineer a sound that was simultaneously disruptive yet undeniably sophisticated. This legacy flows through the birth of jazz and into the digital architecture of hip hop, representing a continuous line of creators who converted their internal mastery into a global currency.

To fully explore this legacy, one must acknowledge the visceral, often carnal origins of the music that followed ragtime. In its infancy, *jazz* was not a term of artistic prestige; it was a slang term for sexual intercourse. It described the kind of wild dancing and uninhibited physical release that respectable society associated with the lower depths of the human expression. To the Victorian moralists of the day, this music was a rhythmic virus, born in the saloons and brothels of the South, designed to erode the character of the American youth.

Yet, a remarkable subversion took place. The very artists who were denigrated as purveyors of vulgarity began to refine their sound with such technical brilliance that the music became undeniable. Figures like Duke Ellington and Louis Armstrong took the raw, kinetic energy of the streets and drafted it into a formal musical language. They engineered a sound that was so infectious and intellectually complex that it eventually bypassed the moral blockades of the era. By the mid-century, the music that was once synonymous with vice had permeated the homes of the very class that had once condemned it. It became the soundtrack of the American home, proving that excellence is the ultimate solvent for prejudice.

This was the same Washingtonian grit Joplin had displayed. These musicians understood that technical mastery was the only way to demand respect in a segregated society. They treated their arrangements as blueprints for a new American classical music. Much like Joplin, they forced the world to acknowledge that their gritty rhythms were actually complex mathematical structures.

The High Priestess and the Fugue: Nina Simone
If any artist embodied the Du Boisian ideal of the Talented Tenth while maintaining the Joplin-esque rigour of classical training, it was Nina Simone. Like Joplin, Simone was a child prodigy who viewed the piano through the lens of Bach and the European canon. Her career was a lifelong refusal to be categorised as a mere entertainer. She infused the jazz and blues traditions with the formal architecture of the fugue and the counterpoint, much like Joplin had done with the rag.

Simone's insistence on being respected as a classical pianist was a direct echo of Joplin's own struggle. She understood that in a society designed to diminish Black intellect, technical mastery was a sovereign act. Her work was not just music; it was a manifestation of human capital used as a weapon for dignity. She proved that the invisible genius could become a visible, vocal force for change without sacrificing an ounce of artistic complexity.

The Architect of the Archive: Michael Jackson
The Washingtonian ideal of economic self-reliance found its most potent late-century reiteration in

Michael Jackson. While often viewed through the lens of pop superstardom, Jackson was a shrewd strategist of intellectual property. He understood a truth that had eluded many of his predecessors: the one who owns the archive owns the future.

His landmark acquisition of the ATV/Beatles catalogue in 1985 was a masterstroke of human capital management. Furthermore, unlike many of his contemporaries, Jackson fought fiercely to retain ownership of his own master recordings. By 2017, his estate stood as a testament to the power of owning one's creative output. He lived out the dream that Joplin had attempted with his own self-publishing ventures, proving that a Black artist could not only dominate the global market but also control its most valuable assets.

The Poet of the Struggle: Tupac Shakur

The link between the Joplin era and the modern era is perhaps most visible in the figure of Tupac Shakur. Both operated within industries that initially sought to market them as simple caricatures; the minstrel for Joplin, and the "thug" for Shakur. Yet, both utilised their platforms to deliver sophisticated, socially conscious messages about literacy and liberation.

Shakur's work, much like *Treemonisha*, was a vision

of survival through knowledge. His "Thug Life" philosophy was, at its core, a call for self-governance and community accountability in the face of systemic neglect. He understood that his voice was his greatest capital. The fact that his music continues to be studied in universities and consumed by middle-class audiences worldwide mirrors the Joplin paradox. It shows that when a creator speaks with enough technical and emotional precision, their message transcends the boundaries of the era that tried to silence them.

The Producer as Architect
The link between Joplin and hip hop is perhaps the most profound in terms of human capital. Joplin was a composer who worked with the limited technology of his time: the piano and the printed score. Modern hip hop producers act as the new architects of the American pulse. They use the digital workstation to engineer rhythms that define global culture.

There is a striking parallel in how both Joplin and hip hop creators have been viewed by the establishment. Both were initially dismissed as creators of a fad. Both were accused of "sampling" or "stealing" from other traditions. Yet, both groups proved that their work required a high order of intellectual labour. A producer like Timberland or

SCOTT JOPLIN: 100 YEARS ON

Dr. Dre operates with the same meticulous attention to tone and timing that Joplin applied to his rags. They are not just making music. They are building a brand through the accumulation of specialised knowledge.

The Paradox of Consumption

Joplin's music was often born in the sporting houses and saloons of the Midwest, yet its largest consumers were middle-class white families with pianos in their sitting rooms. We see this same paradox in hip-hop and rap. A genre that emerged from the urban struggle of the Bronx and Compton is now primarily consumed by white middle-class youth in the suburbs.

This is the "Double-Edged Sword" Joplin knew so well. The music is often celebrated for its "authenticity" or its "edge," even as it is packaged for mass consumption. Hip hop and rap artists today navigate this by being fiercely protective of their business interests. They have learned the lesson Joplin learned the hard way: if you do not own your masters and your publishing, you are merely an entertainer rather than a sovereign creator.

Mapping Modern Sovereignty

As we reflect on the 2017 centenary, Joplin's

greatest gift to modern Black musicians is the concept of self-sovereignty. He proved that an artist could be a philosopher and a strategist as well as a performer. He paved the way for the "Artist-CEO" model that dominates the industry today.

Modern creators no longer wait for institutional permission to be considered geniuses. They follow Joplin's example by building their own platforms and documenting their own excellence. They understand that their creative output is a form of human capital that must be protected and leveraged. Joplin was the first to realise that the most radical act a musician can perform is to claim sovereignty over their pulse. He proved that even when the genius is invisible, the work is eternal.

CHAPTER 9
ARCHIVING THE SILENCE

The centennial revival of the 1970s did more than just restore Scott Joplin's music to the concert hall. It transformed his legacy into a living and breathing mystery. As the centenary of Scott Joplin's demise approaches, the quest for his lost works has entered a new and more urgent phase. History is rarely a completed tapestry. More often, it is a vault where the most vital keys have been systematically misplaced. While we now have the *Maple Leaf Rag* and *Treemonisha*, the full intellectual output of the Invisible Genius remains a fragmented puzzle. The search for the missing manuscripts has moved out of the concert hall and into the realm of forensic investigation. We are no longer merely listeners. We have become the detectives of the archive.

The great tragedy of the archive is not always that things are destroyed. Frequently, they are simply forgotten in the transition between generations. For the researcher in 2017, the hunt for Joplin's lost works is the ultimate high-stakes game of hide and seek. We are searching for the physical ghosts of his later creative thoughts. These are the symphonies that were composed in the shadows of illness. These are the operas that were confiscated by debt.

This chapter explores the researchers who refuse to

let these voices remain silent. It is a story of cold cases and early digital archiving. It is fuelled by the enduring hope that the final piece of the jigsaw is still out there. Perhaps it sits in a dusty attic in Pittsburg, Kansas, or in a discarded pile of legal files in New York. The hunt is an act of historical justice. It is the final step in ensuring that the Invisible Genius is finally seen in his absolute totality as we mark this one-hundredth year since his passing.

The Forensic Historians
The modern researcher relies on a blend of old-world persistence and new-age connectivity. They use the expanding reach of digital databases to track the movement of the Sweatman papers through probate records. This methodology treats the search for the *Symphony No. 1* or *A Guest of Honor* as more than a musical quest. It is a high-stakes game of historical detective work.

The primary challenge lies in the "Sweatman Trail." Because Wilbur Sweatman died without a will in 1961, the physical location of Joplin's manuscripts became a matter of public record but not public access. Forensic historians now spend years cross-referencing auction house catalogues from the 1960s and 1970s. They search for any mention of miscellaneous musical papers or unidentified manuscripts that might have been sold for a pittance to unsuspecting collectors.

Today, the digitisation of state and city archives has provided these detectives with tools that were unavailable to previous generations. They can now trace the addresses of Sweatman's distant relatives with surgical precision. They can identify the specific lawyers involved in the 1960s estate battle. The hope is that one of these legal firms might still hold a "dead file" in a climate-controlled basement. This is a form of archival archaeology. It assumes that the Invisible Genius is not truly gone, but merely buried under the administrative sediment of the twentieth century.

The work is often tedious and unrewarding. It involves scrolling through thousands of pages of microfilm and clicking through countless low-resolution scans of property deeds. Yet, the motivation remains a desire for historical justice. Finding even a single page of the *Symphony No. 1* would represent a massive recovery of intellectual capital. It would prove that Joplin's final years were spent in a state of high-order creative activity rather than just silent decline.

The "Cold Cases" of Ragtime
These are the "cold cases" of American music. One of the most persistent legends involves a trunk

supposedly left in an attic in Pittsburg, Kansas, following the collapse of the *A Guest of Honor* tour in 1903.

Local historians in Kansas have spent decades interviewing the descendants of theatre managers and boarding house owners. They are looking for a heavy, iron-bound trunk that might have been kept as collateral for a debt that was never paid. For avid followers of this story, this trunk is akin to a holy grail. It is a physical symbol of the wealth that was stripped from Joplin during his lifetime.

Another cold case centres on the Manhattan State Hospital. Researchers have attempted to track the personal effects Joplin had with him at the time of his death. While the official records suggest he died penniless, it is possible that he carried a final sketchbook or a collection of musical shorthand. These items would have been of no value to a hospital orderly in 1917. They might have been tucked into a file or claimed by a fellow patient.

Tracking these fragments requires a belief in the "extraordinary prescience" mentioned earlier. It assumes that Joplin left clues behind because he knew we would eventually come looking for them. These cold cases are not just about finding paper. They are about recovering the lost agency of a man who refused to stop composing, even as the world around him went silent.

The Digital Resurrection

Modern technology has begun to offer a new kind of restoration. While we cannot always find the physical manuscripts, we can use digital tools to reconstruct Joplin's intent from the fragments that remain. Researchers are increasingly using music notation software to clean up tattered, low-quality scans of early sheet music. This allows them to identify patterns in his "Invisible Genius" that are invisible to the naked eye.

This is a form of virtual completion. Scholars are beginning to use algorithmic analysis to compare the harmonies of Joplin's late works, such as *Magnetic Rag*, with the few existing themes from his lost opera. By mapping his creative DNA, they can imagine the textures of the symphonies we can no longer hear. While this is not a substitute for the original manuscripts, it is a way of keeping the music alive in the digital age. It represents the potential futuristic frontier of the Joplin legacy. It is an attempt to bridge the gap between the analogue tragedy of the past and the digital possibilities of the future.

The Global Search: Beyond American Borders

The hunt for the Invisible Genius is no longer confined to the American Midwest or the archives of New York. Contemporary researchers have begun to look across the Atlantic. During the early twentieth century, Joplin's music was part of a global phenomenon. The ragtime craze swept through Europe with incredible speed, influencing composers from Debussy to Stravinsky. While Joplin himself never travelled to the grand capitals of Europe, his intellectual capital certainly did.

The theory driving this international search is simple. British and French publishers often licensed or pirated American works to meet the insatiable European demand for syncopated music. It is entirely possible that a copy of a lost rag, or even a fragmented score for *A Guest of Honor*, is sitting in a mislabelled box in the British Library or the Bibliothèque nationale de France. In these vast, ancient repositories, a manuscript might be categorized under "American Popular Song" or "Anonymous Syncopation," waiting for a detective with a trained eye to recognise its true origin.

As we reach the centenary, international digitisation projects are making these distant archives more accessible. We are no longer limited by the physical distance between Texarkana and London. A researcher in a Missouri library can now scan the digital catalogues of European institutions for any trace of the Joplin DNA. This global expansion of the "we" represents the ultimate reach of the Invisible Genius. It suggests that the final piece of the jigsaw might not be found in an American attic, but in a European archive that has held the secret for over a century.

An Enduring Quest

The quest to find the lost Joplin manuscripts is more than a musicological obsession. It is a necessary act of historical restoration. As we mark the 100th year since his passing in 1917, the silence of his missing works remains a profound injustice. Every lost symphony or concerto represents a missing argument for the depth of the Black intellectual tradition. We keep looking because a legacy that is only half-seen is a legacy that is only half-understood.

Finding these works would be the ultimate fulfilment of Joplin's "extraordinary prescience." He trusted that his talent would be recognised by a future generation, and our continued search is the proof of that trust. We are the stewards of his ambition. To find the lost trunk or the confiscated score is to return to Joplin the dignity that the economic and social constraints of his era stripped away. It is an attempt to ensure that the man who died penniless is finally credited with the full wealth of his creative mind.

The search itself has become a form of tribute. Even if the manuscripts are never found, the act of looking acknowledges the weight of what was lost. It confirms that we value his genius enough to never stop searching the shadows of the archive. As the 2017 centenary arrives, we stand as the collective guardians of a masterpiece that is still being recovered. The jigsaw puzzle may remain incomplete for now, but the hunt ensures that the music of Scott Joplin will never again be shrouded in obscurity.

CHAPTER 10

ONE HUNDRED YEARS ON

The message Scott Joplin inscribed into the heart of
Treemonisha in 1911 was never intended as a relic of
the past. It was a living dialogue concerning the
nature of power and the mechanics of freedom. As
we arrive at the centenary of his death in 2017, we
find ourselves in a world that is louder and more
interconnected than any Joplin could have
imagined. Yet, the central question of his "Invisible
Genius" remains more relevant than ever. How
does a marginalised community move from the
periphery of society to the centre of its own destiny?
Joplin's answer was liberation through knowledge.
This principle continues to echo through the
modern pursuit of advancement. It proves that his
vision was not merely for his time, but for all time.

The 2017 Centenary: A Timely Reflection
On 1 April 2017, the clock struck a century since
Scott Joplin was laid to rest in an unmarked grave.
This milestone provides more than just a date for
commemoration. It offers a moment for a long-
overdue intellectual audit. The timing is particularly
poignant. The centenary follows closely on the heels
of the 2016 opening the National Museum of
African American History and Culture (NMAAHC)
in Washington, D.C. This institution represents the
ultimate making visible of the Invisible Genius.

Joplin's legacy is no longer a scattered collection of fragments. It is now anchored in a physical, national landmark that stands within sight of the White House.

It is a historical coincidence that modern research into Joplin's legacy often intersects with other civil rights milestones. The centenary falls in the shadow of the recent anniversaries of the 1965 freedom march from Selma to Montgomery. While the Selma marchers fought for the external right to vote, Joplin's work focused on the internal right to know. In today's fraught and increasingly polarised political landscape, this analysis of Joplin is essential. We must move beyond his reputation as a mere entertainer. To see him only through the lens of ragtime is to miss the political philosopher standing behind the piano. Joplin's life suggests that the ultimate antidote to systemic restriction is not found solely in the halls of government. It is found in the rigorous cultivation of the mind.

Strategy and Activism in the Digital Age

Joplin's era was defined by the competing blueprints for progress offered by Booker T. Washington and W.E.B. Du Bois. In 2017, we find ourselves at a remarkably similar crossroad. The emergence of the *#BlackLivesMatter* movement has utilised digital platforms to bring global attention to systemic issues such as police violence and judicial inequality. This new civil rights movement has prioritised collective action and militant visibility. However, within this activism, the old debates endure.

Some modern strategies focus on external demands, such as calls for reparations or the defunding of traditional institutions. While these movements seek to dismantle barriers from the outside, Joplin's *Treemonisha* offers a different path. His opera suggests that the most durable form of liberation is the acquisition of skills that the market cannot ignore. By 2017, the "knowledge" Joplin fought to spread has been liberated by the internet. Digital archives and sheet music databases have bypassed the gatekeepers of the past. This democratisation of information allows the modern individual to build human capital independently. While modern activism highlights the failures of the state, Joplin highlights the power of the individual to become an institution through technical mastery.

The Economic Argument: Williams and Sowell
The connection between Joplin's vision and modern reality is most visible in the work of economists such as Thomas Sowell and Walter Williams. These thinkers have spent decades arguing that economic literacy is the true foundation of freedom. Williams argued that "In a free society, the most effective way

to eliminate discrimination is to make it costly. When an individual possesses skills that are in high demand, the cost of prejudice becomes an economic burden that few can afford to carry."[4]

This is the exact principle Joplin lived. By mastering the complex structures of grand opera and classical theory, he created a form of wealth that the prejudices of 1917 could not easily confiscate. He understood that a community that produces excellence is a community that cannot be ignored for long. The distinction between political power and economic power is vital here. While 2017 is dominated by debates over legislative changes, Joplin's life was an exercise in radical self-reliance. He believed that excellence was the greatest route to freedom because it was the only asset that was truly portable. In the 21st century, the Invisible Genius serves as a historical case study for this argument. He proves that the accumulation of high-value skills remains a potent shield against any discriminatory landscape.

The William Appling Milestone

As we reach this centenary, the Joplin legacy has achieved a monumental physical milestone. The William Appling Singers and Orchestra have

---

[4] Williams, Walter E. (2011). *Race and Economics: How Much Can Be Blamed on Discrimination?*. Stanford: Hoover Institution Press.

scheduled the release of *Scott Joplin: The Complete Rags, Waltzes & Marches* for 1 April 2017. This project will be the first of its kind. It represents the first time the entire surviving canon has been recorded by an African American conductor and pianist. This is a profound act of cultural reclamation. It ensures that the interpretation of Joplin's work is grounded in the same tradition that birthed it.

As previously noted in our discussion of the opera's legacy, this recording was part of a larger and unfulfilled dream for William Appling. He longed for a grand and definitive staging of *Treemonisha* that would match the scale of the world's greatest opera houses. Appling viewed such a production as the last piece of the jigsaw needed to complete the Joplin legacy. Although he passed away before seeing a modern production reach these heights, his archival work ensures that the blueprints are ready for the next generation.

By placing the complete works into a permanent, high-fidelity archive, Appling's ensemble have secured a vital portion of the American cultural record. They have ensured that Joplin's intellectual property is no longer a collection of scattered fragments, but a unified body of work that can be continuously studied and performed.

The Human Spirit and the Unfinished Legacy

The core thesis of Scott Joplin's life is that the human spirit, fired by expressions of creativity, provides the ultimate motivation for liberation. His opera was a triumph of hope over experience. It offered a vision of a progressive future that remains as necessary today as it was in 1911. We keep looking at Joplin because his life confirms that the genius within every individual is the greatest threat to a stagnant society.

The spotlight has finally returned to Scott Joplin. However, the work of liberation through knowledge remains an urgent pursuit. As we conclude this reflection on a century of progress, we must acknowledge that the legacy is still unfinished. The blueprints are in our hands. The rhythm of his persistence is in our ears. The task of the next century is not just to remember his music. It is to embody the excellence he demanded of himself. The Invisible Genius has finally been seen. Now, we must ensure his message is acted upon.

CHAPTER 11

THE SOVEREIGN PULSE

On 1 April 2017, the world marks precisely one century since Scott Joplin drew his final breath in a quiet ward on Ward's Island. For much of that hundred-year span, the silence surrounding his name was literal. His scores sat in dusty trunks and his name was a fading echo in the halls of popular music. Yet, as we stand at this centennial vantage point, it is clear that the Invisible Genius has finally achieved a state of permanent visibility. No longer a ghost haunting the archives of American history, Joplin has become one of its most structural pillars.

The Century of Persistence

The century following 1917 represents a profound triumph of merit over circumstance. Joplin's life was a battle against the shrouds of obscurity, yet his music acted as a silent ambassador for his intellect. Even when the composer was forgotten, the compositions refused to die. They survived the transition from piano rolls to shellac discs, and from vinyl to the digital streams of 2017.

This persistence is the ultimate validation of Joplin's artistic philosophy. He believed that high-quality work would eventually force the market to prioritise excellence over personal bias. The century between his death and this centenary has proven him correct. Ragtime did not remain a populist fad of the 1890s. It evolved into a formalised language of American classical music. Joplin's journey from an unmarked pauper's grave to the Pulitzer Prize is the definitive narrative of the twentieth century. It is a story of a man whose human capital was so vast that not even death could keep it suppressed.

The Model of the Creator-Entrepreneur

As we look toward the next century, Joplin serves as a vital model for the modern creator. He was a multi-media freelancer long before the term existed. He navigated various projects and platforms, from sheet music publishing to grand opera production. His life demonstrates that the acquisition of high-value skills is the most portable and universally recognised form of currency.

In his 2011 seminal work *Race and Economics*, Walter Williams highlights how productivity acts as a shield in a discriminatory landscape. Joplin's life is the historical proof of this modern economic theory. He did not just write melodies; he built intellectual property. He fought for royalties and insisted on the dignity of his craft at every turn. Today new generations of creators navigate an increasingly complex digital landscape, Joplin's commitment to his work offers a timeless blueprint. He proves that technical mastery is a shield against social restriction. His legacy is a reminder that while markets may fluctuate, the value of undeniable talent remains a constant.

The Invisible Genius Made Manifest

The primary achievement of the last century has been the unveiling of the man behind the music. We have moved beyond the caricature of the "ragtime professor" to recognise the cerebral architect of a national sound. The efforts of the 1970s revivalists and the modern archival detectives have turned the Invisible Genius into a tangible historical figure.

We now see Joplin as he saw himself: a leader who sought to free his community from poverty through the power of art. The designation of his St. Louis home as a National Historic Landmark and the posthumous honours from the musical establishment are more than just accolades. They are the physical manifestations of a restored dignity. The "we" of 2017; the listeners, readers, archivists, historians, and musicians, have successfully reclaimed the narrative. We have ensured that the tragic silence of his final years was a temporary state, not a permanent conclusion.

The Horizon of 2117

What will the Joplin legacy look like when the bicentenary arrives in 2117? The hope for the next hundred years is that the missing pieces of the jigsaw will finally be found. The search for the lost manuscripts is the unfinished business of our generation. We look forward to a future where the *Symphony No. 1* and *A Guest of Honor* are not just titles in a catalogue, but living performances in our concert halls.

The next century will likely see Joplin's influence expand even further beyond the borders of the United States. As global culture becomes increasingly syncopated, his role as the "King of Ragtime" will be seen as the starting point for a worldwide musical revolution. He was the first to prove that the rhythms of the African-American experience could be translated into the formal language of global high art. In 2117, he will likely be recognised not just as an American master, but as a foundational figure in the history of world music.

The Persistence Of Genius
Success, as Frederick Douglass argued, is not a gift of chance but an attribute of power derived from self-mastery. Joplin's life was the ultimate manifestation of this principle. He did not merely survive a hostile era; he engineered a legacy that was designed to outlast it. He understood that while his physical self was subject to the limitations of his

time, the disciplined architecture of his mind was sovereign.

The journey from the racy saloons of the Midwest to the hallowed stage of the Metropolitan Opera represents the great correction of American history. It is the moment when the invisible genius was finally assigned his true value. We have seen how Joplin's human capital, his meticulous notation, his formal training, and his unwavering belief in the power of literacy paved the way for Black creators who followed. From the high-art fusions of Nina Simone to the strategic ownership of Michael Jackson, the Joplin blueprint remains the gold standard for artistic sovereignty.

Joplin's music remains a rhythmic argument for dignity. It is a reminder that excellence is a universal solvent for prejudice. By becoming his own master through his art, Scott Joplin did more than just write the soundtrack for an era. He proved that even when the manuscripts are missing and the stage is dark, a master of himself can never truly be silenced. The shroud of obscurity has finally lifted, revealing a legacy that was built not just for a hundred years, but for the ages.

THE COMPLETE WORKS OF SCOTT JOPLIN

To truly grasp the magnitude of the Invisible Genius, one must look beyond the handful of melodies that have permeated popular culture. Joplin was a prolific and disciplined architect of sound. His output represents a tireless investment in his own human capital, spanning from sentimental ballads to the sophisticated and multi-layered structures of grand opera. For many, the sheer scale of his output remains a surprise. To understand the depth of his labour, one must look at the breadth of his catalogue.

This appendix presents a comprehensive and unified chronology of his creative output, going beyond the surviving canon to include works known only through copyright records, contemporary advertisements, or rediscovered piano rolls. It serves as the ultimate record of a man who, even in his final years of physical decline, never ceased his intellectual labour.

The Final Tally of a Genius

To the newcomer, this list is an invitation to explore a world far richer than *The Sting* might suggest. To the avid fan, it is a reminder of why we continue to search the archives. Each "LOST" marker is a challenge to the future; each surviving score is a victory for the human spirit. Joplin left us with not only melodies, but a roadmap for excellence that we are still learning to follow.

Legend:
Standard Text: Surviving published work.
Italics with Asterisk (*): Lost or unpublished work.
[PR]: Rediscovered piano roll (transcribed and published posthumously).

The Master List (1894–1917)

Year	Title	Genre	Notes
1894	A Picture of Her Face	Song	First published composition
1894	On the Levee	Song	
1895	Please Say You Will	Song	
1896	Combination March	March	
1896	Harmony Club Waltz	Waltz	
1896	The Great Crush Collision March	March	
1899	**Maple Leaf Rag**	Piano Rag	The work that defined the genre
1899	Original Rags	Piano Rag	Arranged by Charles N. Daniels
1900	Swipesy Cake Walk	Piano Rag	Written with Arthur Marshall
1901	Augustan Club Waltz	Waltz	

Year	Title	Genre	Notes
1901	I Am Thinking of My Pickaninny Days	Song	Reflects the era's commercial "coon song" tropes
1901	Peacherine Rag	Piano Rag	
1901	Sunflower Slow Drag	Piano Rag	Written with Scott Hayden
1901	The Easy Winners	Piano Rag	
1901	*A Blizzard**	Piano Rag	**LOST**
1902	A Breeze from Alabama	Piano Rag	
1902	Cleopha	March/Two-Step	
1902	Elite Syncopations	Piano Rag	
1902	March Majestic	March	
1902	**The Entertainer**	Piano Rag	Joplin's most enduring global melody
1902	The Ragtime Dance	Song/Dance	First version (included vocal cues)
1902	The Strenuous Life	Piano Rag	Tribute to Theodore Roosevelt
1903	***A Guest of Honor****	**Opera**	**LOST** (Confiscated for debts in Kansas)
1903	*Dude's Parade**	Orchestral	**LOST** (From *A Guest of Honor*)
1903	Little Black Baby	Song	
1903	Palm Leaf Rag	Piano Rag	
1903	*Patriotic Patrol**	Orchestral	**LOST** (From *A Guest of Honor*)
1903	Something Doing	Piano Rag	Written with Scott

Year	Title	Genre	Notes
			Hayden
1903	Weeping Willow	Piano Rag	
1904	Cascades	Piano Rag	Inspired by the St. Louis World's Fair
1904	The Chrysanthemum	Piano Rag	
1904	The Favorite	Piano Rag	
1904	The Sycamore	Piano Rag	
1905	Bethena	Concert Waltz	Written following the death of his second wife
1905	Binks' Waltz	Waltz	
1905	Leola	Piano Rag	
1905	Rosebud March	March	
1905	Sarah Dear	Song	
1905	*You Stand Good with Me, Babe**	Song	**LOST**
1906	Antoinette	March/Two-Step	
1906	Eugenia	Piano Rag	
1906	*Good-bye Old Gal Goodbye**	Song	**LOST**
1906	The Ragtime Dance	Piano Rag	Simplified piano-only version
1907	Gladiolus Rag	Piano Rag	
1907	Heliotrope Bouquet	Piano Rag	Written with Louis Chauvin
1907	Lily Queen	Piano Rag	Written with Arthur Marshall
1907	Nonpareil (None to Equal)	Piano Rag	

Year	Title	Genre	Notes
1907	Rose Leaf Rag	Piano Rag	
1907	Searchlight Rag	Piano Rag	
1907	Snoring Sampson	Song	Subtitled "A Quarrel in Ragtime"
1907	*When Your Hair Is Like the Snow**	Song	**LOST**
1908	Fig Leaf Rag	Piano Rag	
1908	Pine Apple Rag	Piano Rag	
1908	School of Ragtime	Educational	Six exercises for piano
1908	Sensation	Piano Rag	Composed by Joseph Lamb; Arranged by Joplin
1908	Sugar Cane	Piano Rag	
1909	Country Club	Piano Rag	
1909	Euphonic Sounds	Piano Rag	
1909	Paragon Rag	Piano Rag	
1909	Pleasant Moments	Ragtime Waltz	
1909	Solace	Mexican Serenade	Joplin's venture into Habanera rhythms
1909	Wall Street Rag	Piano Rag	
1910	Pine Apple Rag	Song	Vocal version with lyrics by Joplin
1910	Stoptime Rag	Piano Rag	Instructs the performer to tap their foot
1911	Felicity Rag	Piano Rag	Written with Scott Hayden
1911	*Lovin' Babe**	Piano Rag	**LOST**

Year	Title	Genre	Notes
1911	**Treemonisha**	**Opera**	Joplin's magnum opus; self-published score
1912	Scott Joplin's New Rag	Piano Rag	
1913	Kismet Rag	Piano Rag	Written with Scott Hayden
1914	Magnetic Rag	Piano Rag	His final published rag; self-published
1914	**Silver Swan Rag [PR]**	Piano Rag	Rediscovered via piano roll; published 1971
1915	*Frolic of the Bears**	Dance	**LOST** (Likely an addition to *Treemonisha*)
1915	*Morning Glories**	Piano Rag	**LOST**
1915	*Syncopated Jamboree**	Vaudeville	**LOST**
1915	*Pretty Pansy Rag**	Piano Rag	**LOST**
1915	*Recitative Rag**	Piano Rag	**LOST**
1915	*For the Sake of All**	Song	**LOST**
1915	*If**	Song	**LOST**
1916	***Symphony No. 1****	**Symphony**	**LOST** (Mentioned in correspondence)
1916	***Piano Concerto****	**Concerto**	**LOST**
1917	Reflection Rag	Piano Rag	Published posthumously by John Stark

This chronology is a challenge to the future. Every work marked as LOST represents a gap in our collective cultural heritage. As we enter the next century of Scott Joplin's legacy, let these titles stand as a testament to a mind that refused to be obscured.

A Note on the Sources

The genesis of this work lies in a conversation with Hugh C. Shields, who first proposed the idea of a centennial book on Scott Joplin. As I immersed myself in his history, I was struck by something far more profound than a standard biography could capture. I found a man whose strategic approach to his craft offered a masterclass in resilience. This legacy holds startling relevance for the contemporary advocate of Black sovereignty. Joplin's life serves as a philosophical case study in the power of self-mastery as a prerequisite for true freedom.

In constructing this narrative, I relied on the foundational research of Edward A. Berlin. His 1994 biography, *King of Ragtime: Scott Joplin and His Era*, remains the definitive account of the composer's life. Berlin's meticulous archival work recovered lost performance dates and traced the failed tours of Joplin's opera companies. He also documented the cold reality of the 1915 *Treemonisha* read-through. These findings provided the essential empirical scaffolding for the "Invisible Genius" framework.

However, the interpretation of these facts through the lens of Human Capital and Pragmatic Conservatism are my own. While Berlin provided the history, this essay provides the philosophy of that history. This specific angle of Joplin as a navigator of his own destiny through a form of radical, pragmatic autonomy had remained largely unexplored in existing literature. It was this void that I sought to fill.

By placing Joplin's career in direct dialogue with the intellectual crossroads of Booker T. Washington and W.E.B. Du Bois, I aimed to show that Joplin was not merely a subject of his era. He was a sovereign actor within it. His decision to self-publish, his insistence on classical tempo markings, and his transition into grand opera are treated here as deliberate acts of intellectual sovereignty. This book builds upon the scholarly consensus to argue that Joplin's greatest work was not just the music itself. It was the meticulous documentation of a mind that refused to be obscured. My aim was to bring his story to life in a way that resonates with the challenges of our world today.

Sarah Peace

BIBLIOGRAPHY

Primary Sources: Writings and Correspondence

Douglass, Frederick. *Self-Made Men.* Edited by John W. Blassingame. New York: Library of America, 1994 (Originally delivered as a lecture in 1872).

Du Bois, W.E.B. *The Souls of Black Folk.* Chicago: A.C. McClurg & Co., 1903.

Joplin, Scott. *Treemonisha: Opera in Three Acts.* New York: Scott Joplin, 1911 (Vocal Score).

Washington, Booker T. *Up From Slavery: An Autobiography.* New York: Doubleday, 1901.

Washington, Booker T. "The Atlanta Exposition Address." September 18, 1895. In *The Booker T. Washington Papers,* edited by Louis R. Harlan. Urbana: University of Illinois Press, 1974.

Primary Sources: Musical Scores and Archives

Joplin, Scott. *Maple Leaf Rag.* Sedalia, MO: John Stark & Son, 1899.

Joplin, Scott. *The Strenuous Life: A Ragtime Two-Step.* St. Louis: John Stark & Son, 1902.

Joplin, Scott. *A Guest of Honor.* (Lost Manuscript). Originally registered for copyright, 1903.

Joplin, Scott. *Magnetic Rag.* New York: Scott Joplin Music Publishing Co., 1914.

Secondary Sources: Biographies and Musical Scholarship

Berlin, Edward A. *King of Ragtime: Scott Joplin and His Era.* New York: Oxford University Press, 1994. (The foundational source for this text).

Berlin, Edward A. *Ragtime: A Musical and Cultural History.* Berkeley: University of California Press, 1980.

Blesh, Rudi, and Harriet Janis. *They All Played Ragtime.* New York: Alfred A. Knopf, 1950.

Curtis, Susan. *Dancing to a Black Man's Tune: A Life of Scott Joplin.* Columbia: University of Missouri Press, 1994.

Haskins, James, and Kathleen Benson. *Scott Joplin.* New York: Doubleday, 1978.

Schafer, William J., and Johannes Riedel. *The Art of Ragtime: Form and Meaning of an Original Black American Art.* Baton Rouge: Louisiana State University Press, 1973.

Modern Reception and Cultural Context

Appling, William. *Scott Joplin: The Complete Piano Works.* Albany Records, 2017 (Posthumous release/Liner notes).

Giddins, Gary. *Visions of Jazz: The First Century.* New York: Oxford University Press, 1998.

Schuller, Gunther. *Early Jazz: Its Roots and Musical Development.* New York: Oxford University Press, 1968.

Tate, Greg. *Everything but the Burden: What White People Are Taking from Black Culture.* New York: Broadway Books, 2003. (Contextualising the "Vice to Virtue" paradox).

Legal and Historical Context

Harlan, Louis R. *Booker T. Washington: The Making of a Black Leader, 1856–1901.* New York: Oxford University Press, 1972.

Litwack, Leon F. *Trouble in Mind: Black Southerners in the Age of Jim Crow.* New York: Alfred A. Knopf, 1998.

Plessy v. Ferguson, 163 U.S. 537 (1896).

Scott Joplin
(24 November 1868 – 1 April 1917)

A restored portrait first appearing in the *St. Louis Globe-Democrat*, 7 June 1903.

Source: U.S. Library of Congress.

www.ingramcontent.com/pod-product-compliance
Lightning Source LLC
Chambersburg PA
CBHW020955030426
42339CB00005B/106